LIVING WITH
DISORDERS AND
DISABILITIES

LIVING WITH
PHOBIAS

by Heidi Ayarbe

ReferencePoint
Press®

San Diego, CA

For more information, contact:
ReferencePoint Press, Inc.
PO Box 27779
San Diego, CA 92198
www.ReferencePointPress.com

LIBRARY OF CONGRESS CATALOGING-IN-PUBLICATION DATA

Name: Ayarbe, Heidi, author.
Title: Living with Phobias / by Heidi Ayarbe.
Description: San Diego, CA : ReferencePoint Press, Inc., [2019] | Series:
    Living with Disorders and Disabilities | Audience: Grade 9 to 12. |
    Includes bibliographical references and index.
Identifiers: LCCN 2018011540 (print) | LCCN 2018011767 (ebook) | ISBN
    9781682824887 (ebook) | ISBN 9781682824870 (hardback : alk. paper)
Subjects: LCSH: Phobias—Juvenile literature. | Phobias—Treatment—Juvenile
    literature. | Panic disorders—Treatment—Juvenile literature.
Classification: LCC RC535 (ebook) | LCC RC535 .A95 2019 (print) | DDC
    616.85/225—dc23
LC record available at https://lccn.loc.gov/2018011540

CONTENTS

Introduction
Ryan and Martina   4

Chapter 1
What Are Phobias?   10

Chapter 2
Diagnosing Phobias   26

Chapter 3
How Do Phobias Affect
Daily Life?   44

Chapter 4
Beyond Fear   58

Source Notes   70
For Further Research   74
Index   76
Image Credits   79
About the Author   80

INTRODUCTION

RYAN AND MARTINA

Martina felt sick when she woke up. In fact, she hadn't slept very well. When her parents surprised the family with a spring break vacation, everybody had celebrated. Her brothers spent the night packing, trying to decide how many pairs of swim shorts they needed. They argued about who'd get the window seat on the plane. But Martina didn't want to think about the plane. She felt a familiar sense of dread.

Everyone bustled with energy the morning of the trip, but Martina could barely swallow her breakfast. Her parents made a comment that Martina was just too excited to eat.

Her family arrived at the airport. They walked through the terminal. All around Martina, other travelers laughed and talked. She wondered how they made life look so easy. After the family arrived at the gate, Martina's heart began to pound. She could see planes taxiing out the windows. Her ears burned. Everything blurred and shifted out of focus. Martina looked at the ground. She tried to focus on the weird carpet pattern.

Many people are afraid of flying. But an irrational fear of flying might be a specific phobia.

Her brothers laughed and chased each other, but Martina sat in the closest seat and tried to focus on her breathing. Martina's mom showed her a travel brochure with a photograph of a girl horseback riding on the beach. She asked if Martina would like to do that. Martina opened her mouth to speak, but she couldn't say anything. She just nodded up and down, hoping her mother wouldn't ask any more questions.

Their boarding group was called. Martina felt like everything inside her was electric. The electricity moved to her heart and lungs, tightening around them like ropes. Her vision was splotchy and her breathing shallow. She felt like she didn't control her body anymore. And the worst part was while she struggled to get control of her body, she was flooded with shame. Normal teenagers weren't afraid of flying.

Ryan's Story

Ryan's throat tightened as he watched his friends head to the mall elevator. He insisted that they take the stairs to get some exercise, but his friends were laughing and messing around, not paying attention to him. Everybody piled into the elevator. Ryan didn't want to stand out and take the stairs alone, but he was afraid of joining them in the elevator.

"Come on!" his friend Justin said. Ryan felt like he didn't have a choice, so he got in. He stood near the elevator doors and took deep breaths. He focused on the digital floor number that popped up on the control panel. When the doors opened on the second floor, more people pushed in. They shoved Ryan away from the doors.

Ryan trembled all over. The elevator got hot, too hot. It felt like he was suffocating. His friends' laughter seemed miles away. A tingling overtook his body.

When the doors opened again, he pushed through the crowded elevator and shot out of the door. Sweat dripped down his temples. He leaned over, steadying himself, trying to ease his breathing.

The Fear Factor

Both Ryan and Martina were experiencing fear. According to the *Diagnostic and Statistical Manual of Mental Disorders, Fifth Edition* (*DSM-5*), fear is an "emotional response to a real or perceived imminent threat," that everyone experiences from time to time.[1] Fear is a necessary survival tool for keeping us safe. Dr. Thierry Steimer, a professor who works with the Clinical Psychopharmacology Unit at the Geneva University Hospital, explains, "The main function of fear . . . is to act as a signal of danger, threat, or motivational conflict, and to trigger appropriate adaptive responses."[2]

For instance, we might feel afraid when we are lost on a dark street. Fear kicks our body into an alert mode, making us more aware and more focused. There might be dangerous things lurking in the dark. An adaptive response might be to turn around or light the street with a flashlight. Similarly, if we see a big dog running toward us, our appropriate adaptive response might be to call for help.

But Ryan and Martina aren't experiencing appropriate responses. They have specific phobias, or "strong irrational fear reactions" to objects or situations, according to the Anxiety and Depression Association of America (ADAA). Ryan has claustrophobia, or a phobia of small spaces. Martina has a phobia of flying. Phobias, instead of helping us survive, can limit our actions. People with phobias often go to extreme lengths to avoid the objects, or *phobic stimuli*, that frighten them.

Avoidance may seem rational and non-problematic. If someone is afraid of snakes and lives in a big city, chances are that she'll never have to confront the phobia. But avoidance can have some pretty extreme repercussions. Think of Martina's reaction to a fun family vacation, which might affect where she can travel. Or Ryan's

> "The main function of fear . . . is to act as a signal of danger, threat, or motivational conflict, and to trigger appropriate adaptive responses."[2]
>
> —Dr. Thierry Steimer, professor

claustrophobia, which might interfere with the types of buildings he feels comfortable in. Phobias, though seemingly benign, can change the course of someone's life. An anonymous reader with a phobia of flying wrote into an advice column in the *Guardian* about this exact problem:

> [I am] due to be interviewed for a dream role within an international company. The role is based at its worldwide HQ but it has offices all around the world. The problem is I have a fear of flying. In the past this has lost me several other roles. . . . What should I do? Be upfront and risk not getting the job again? Or say nothing and risk losing the job once I start it?[3]

"In the past [my fear of flying] has lost me several other roles. . . . What should I do? Be upfront and risk not getting the job again? Or say nothing and risk losing the job once I start it?"[3]

—*Anonymous contributor, the* Guardian

Though many people with phobias might get through life by accommodating their lifestyles to avoid their phobic stimuli, others may face real-world consequences. They could lose the opportunity to grow in their career, or even be fired from their job, as in the example above.

The ADAA states that "specific phobias affect 19 million adults, or 8.7% of the U.S. population."[4] Many phobias develop suddenly during early childhood, when people are unable to remember the cause of the phobia. Some situational phobias, such as a fear of flying, can develop during adolescence and early adulthood. The phobic stimulus might even be something that previously did not induce a

Mental health providers diagnose phobias using the *DSM-5*.
This keeps diagnoses consistent from provider to provider.

fear response. Yet people tend to avoid the stimuli rather than seek professional treatment. According to the ADAA, "only 36.9% of those suffering receive treatment."[5]

Phobias are often misunderstood and brushed off as being frivolous. But phobias are real and can be quite powerful, affecting someone's life in a myriad of ways. By understanding phobias, teens can practice techniques to reduce anxiety and better manage their phobias.

Chapter 1

WHAT ARE PHOBIAS?

Though Martina and Ryan are not real people, their stories are all too common for people with phobias. Specific phobia is an anxiety disorder similar in classification to generalized anxiety disorder, separation anxiety disorder, and panic disorder, among others. Most phobias are of specific objects or situations, and many people with phobias can have multiple specific phobias. Regardless of the stressor, phobias induce fear or anxiety, the anticipation of encountering the phobia, in the people who have them.

What Is the Difference between Fear and Phobia?

Certainly, it's not uncommon for someone to say she is afraid of something, whether it be of small spaces, spiders, or heights. It would probably be safe to say that everyone has experienced a fear response at some point in their life. But just because someone has experienced a fear response, it doesn't mean that person suffers from a phobia.

Professors Carlos Coehlo and Helena Purkis, from the University of Queensland, write that "fears are quick and adaptive responses that permit powerful reply to imminent threats. . . . [Phobias] are extreme manifestations of fear to objects or situations in the absence of a proportional danger."[6] In other words, the main difference between healthy fear and phobia is that someone who has a phobia can't control his fear response, even though he may be aware the fear is irrational. Even thinking about the feared object or situation can send him into fight-flight-freeze mode.

> **"Fears are quick and adaptive responses that permit powerful reply to imminent threats. . . . [Phobias] are extreme manifestations of fear to objects or situations in the absence of a proportional danger."[5]**
>
> —*Carlos Coehlo and Helena Purkis, professors, University of Queensland*

Fight-flight-freeze is a mechanism that helps the body cope with stress and fear. It is automatic and cannot be controlled. Breathing increases, as does heart rate. The body prepares to run away from the threat or face it head on. But sometimes the threat is intense enough that the body doesn't know what to do. Sometimes it "freezes" and gets overwhelmed. This might cause tension in the muscles. But regardless of whether the body decides to fight, flee, or freeze, all of the reactions are a response to fear.

Fear is essential to survival. From a physiological point of view, fear is not a choice. Allen Shawn, author of *Wish I Could Be There: Notes from a Phobic Life,* says, "It is the sympathetic nervous system,

People with a phobia of heights may experience extreme fear when faced with a cliff or sudden drop. This fear might keep them from outdoor activities.

triggered by the inner brain's instructions, that manufactures the physiology of anxiety and fear."[7] To better understand phobias and how the body reacts during an acute fear response, it's important to understand the physiology of fear and *why* the body seems to take over on its own accord.

The Physiology of Fear

Everyone has different fears. Someone might feel afraid when walking home along a dark street. Someone might feel afraid when a thunderstorm rattles the bedroom window. Someone might feel afraid after almost being hit by a car in an intersection. Though what people

Scared Stiff

The expression "scared stiff" is common, but for years scientists were baffled as to why some people, during moments of intense threat, seemed paralyzed with fear. In 2014, neuroscientists at the University of Bristol might have discovered why.

Researchers discovered a pathway between a region in the brain called the periaqueductal gray (PAG) to a part of the brain that controls movement, the pyramis. The PAG is a mid-brain region that is important for controlling pain and plays a significant role in anxiety and fear. The pyramis generates freezing behavior when an animal is under intense threat. For instance, an animal that has no escape will stand still in an effort to not be detected, in effect, playing dead. This freezing makes someone physiologically "scared stiff."

People also call this a "deer in headlights," because deer often freeze when approached by an oncoming car. However, the deer are not experiencing the same paralysis from the PAG. The pupils of deer dilate to maximize vision at dawn and dusk, adjusting to the low light. Imagine sitting in a dark room when someone turns on the lights. You probably shade your eyes until they adjust. When deer find themselves facing a pair of headlights, pupils dilated, they cannot see anything. So they freeze, so to speak, until they can see—which is often too late.

fear differs, the way the human body reacts to fear is very much the same. Someone gripped by fear might experience a clenched gut, a tightening in the chest and throat, trembling hands, shortness of breath, numbness, or tingling. Each of these descriptions touches on different aspects of the biochemistry of fear. Because the brain acts in such a complex way, scientists continually research the brain to try to decipher its complexities. There are many parts of the brain involved in fear.

The fear response is believed to begin in the amygdala. The amygdala is the part of the brain that detects the emotional salience of the object causing fear. Salience is a way to describe how much

FEAR AND THE BRAIN

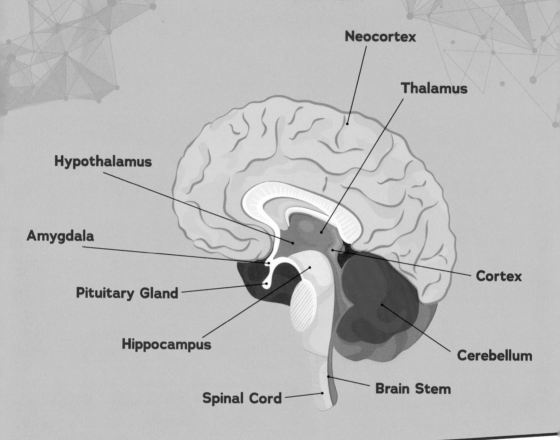

Neocortex

Thalamus

Hypothalamus

Amygdala

Cortex

Pituitary Gland

Hippocampus

Cerebellum

Spinal Cord

Brain Stem

Many parts of the brain play a role in the fear response. Fear signals travel through the body by the brain stem, which is connected to the spinal cord. When the hypothalamus activates the fight-flight-freeze response, the adrenal glands (located on top of the kidneys) release epinephrine, which increases breathing and heart rate. Then, the hypothalamus and pituitary gland signal the adrenal glands to release cortisol, which puts the body on high alert. The hippocampus can decide to continue the fear response, or it can relax the body if the threat is not real.

one thing stands out to us, relative to its neighbors. This goes for all emotions, but it is always more pronounced with anger or fear. First a person sees, or perceives, a threat. Once the threat is registered, conscious thought shuts down.

According to Arash Javanbakht and Linda Saab, Assistant Professors of Psychiatry at Wayne State University, "a threat stimulus . . . triggers a fear response in the amygdala, which activates areas involved in preparation for motor functions involved in fight or flight."[9] The chain reaction continues with the thalamus, which is part of the limbic system. The thalamus processes the incoming sensory data. Based on that data, the hypothalamus decides whether the threat is real. The fight-flight-freeze response then activates accordingly.

An article in *Harvard Health* further explains the biological process. When the hypothalamus activates the fight-flight-freeze response, "these [adrenal] glands respond by pumping the hormone epinephrine (also known as adrenaline) into the bloodstream. As epinephrine circulates through the body, it brings a number of physiological changes."[9] The heart beats faster, which causes the pulse and blood pressure to increase. This can cause trembling hands and shortness of breath. Small airways in the lungs open so the brain gets extra oxygen and becomes more alert, focusing on the threat. Finally, epinephrine triggers the release of stored sugars and fats, which flood the bloodstream and prepare the body with enough energy to react.

This primary fear response happens within seconds, and we are not consciously aware of it happening. Fear is instinctive and primal, and often we can't control it. But the body's not done yet. After the surge of epinephrine subsides, the body begins with stage two of the fear response, known as the HPA axis. The hypothalamus, pituitary gland, and adrenal glands prompt the release of cortisol. Cortisol keeps the body on high alert.

Finally, conscious thought kicks in. When the hippocampus receives the messages from the amygdala, it helps the brain decide whether the threat is real or not. Think of that initial surge of panic you might feel when someone jumps out and shouts, "Boo!" The extreme reaction quickly subsides when the hippocampus receives the messages because it can establish context. The emotional response we feel keeps us alert and focused on the threat, or, on the other hand, it can click our bodies back into relaxation.

When somebody is living with a phobia, even thinking about the phobia can create an emotional response that doesn't fit the situation. The hippocampus might not establish necessary context. The threat persists, so the body continues to experience the fear response.

Millions of Years of History in 3 Pounds

The human brain weighs approximately 3 pounds (1.4 kg). These 3 pounds are the control center of the entire body. The Mayo Clinic website explains that the "brain contains billions of nerve cells arranged in patterns that coordinate thought, emotion, behavior, movement and sensation."[10] The anatomy of the brain—its folds, wrinkles, nested structures, and overlapping parts—continues to fascinate and perplex scientists. Cracking the mysteries of the brain will take lifetimes.

Nevertheless, the more neuroscientists, neurologists, psychiatrists, biologists, and geneticists study the brain, the more they understand

Preparing a meal uses both unconscious and conscious responses. Deciding what to cook for dinner is conscious. Moving your hand away from the hot stove is unconscious.

fear and phobias. In a *Discover* article titled "Fear in the Brain," author Stephen Johnson writes:

> *[Scientists] have learned that fear plays tricks with our memory and our perception of reality. . . . the fear systems in the brain have their own perceptual channels and their own dedicated circuitry for storing traumatic memories. As scientists have mapped the path of fear through the brain, they have begun to explore ways to lessen its hold on the psyche, to prevent that*

car accident from keeping us off the road months later.[11]

To better understand the physiology of fear and how it works in the body, we have to take a trip back in time.

The Triune Brain Theory

American physician and neuroscientist Dr. Paul D. MacLean changed the way we understand the brain when he proposed the *triune brain* theory in the 1960s. He divided the brain into three regions: the reptilian, paleomammalian, and neomammalian complexes. Despite receiving criticism for being overly simplistic, his theory is useful as an approximation to understanding the mysteries of the brain. MacLean's theory established that some brain functions are older, from an evolutionary standpoint, than others.

John Hawks, a professor of anthropology at the University of Wisconsin–Madison, writes that "across nearly seven million years, the human brain has tripled in size, with most of this growth occurring in the past two million years. . . . [For] the first two thirds of our history, the size of our ancestors' brains was within the range of those of other apes living today."[12]

Hawks is only talking about contemporary history. The brain dates back hundreds of millions of years. The earliest form of the brain is often called the reptilian brain. It is comprised of the brain stem region and cerebellum. This part of the brain first appeared more than 500 million years ago and reached its most advanced stage approximately 250 million years ago.

The newer parts of the brain developed with mammals approximately 150 million years ago. They contain the hypothalamus, amygdala, and hippocampus. Professor Hawks says that "[t]he final third of our evolution saw nearly all the action in brain size, including an expansion of a language-connected part of the frontal lobe called Broca's area."[13] This is the cortex and neocortex, which make possible language, culture, abstract thought, and imagination. This part of the brain has infinite possibilities to grow and learn. It's not stuck in time.

During moments of threat and fear, the neocortex and cortex, along with the hippocampus, work to give the brain context and control. This helps the body react appropriately to fear and to adjust the response if necessary.

The Brain's Two Roads of Fear

In the 1980s, postdoctoral student Joseph LeDoux discovered something important about fear and danger. Fear, threats, and danger follow two pathways in the brain. One is primal and instinctive. LeDoux called this the low-road of fear. It includes the amygdala, which kicks in the fight-flight-freeze response. The other pathway is conscious and rational. LeDoux called it the high-road of fear. It includes the cortex and neocortex, which analyze the incoming data. In every instance where fear is perceived, the brain sends information down the two roads. In his article, Johnson explains:

The key difference between the two paths is data transmission time. It might take a few seconds to establish the presence of [a threat like] the snake and formulate a response via the high road, but the low road kicks the body into a freezing response within a fraction of a second. And you don't have to learn the elaborate bodily choreography involved, the way you might learn a complicated yoga position. Your body knows how to execute the freezing response without any training at all. In fact, it knows the response so well that it is nearly impossible to keep it from happening."[14]

The fear response is so integral to survival that some scientists believe that the human fear system has evolved over millions of years to keep us safe from threats from early in our evolutionary history, such as snakes, spiders, heights, small spaces, and open spaces. This evolution of fear has been imprinted on our amygdala, and it has yet to catch up with technology. Johnson further says, "The fact that the amygdala's basic architecture reappears in so many species is testimony to its evolutionary importance: Natural selection generally doesn't tinker with components that have proved essential to basic survival."[15]

> **"Natural selection generally doesn't tinker with components that have proved essential to basic survival."**[15]
>
> —Stephen Johnson, author of "Fear in the Brain."

Because of the way our brains are wired, the amygdala does not want to let go of the fear response. It wants to keep us alive. This fear response, now seemingly etched on the brain, can be devastating for people like Martina and Ryan. Martina will do anything she can to avoid getting on a plane. Ryan's elevator panic attack means he's likely going to choose to take the stairs next time. Neither of these things are immediately dangerous, but going unchecked, these phobias can spiral into life-limiting realities. Ryan might not take a job on the top floor of a skyscraper to avoid getting in an elevator. Martina could miss out on opportunities to travel and experience interesting things because she will refuse to fly.

There are three anxiety disorders that use the term *phobia* to describe the intense fear experienced by the person with the phobia: agoraphobia, social phobia (also known as social anxiety disorder, or SAD), and specific phobia. It's important to understand the differences, as well as the similarities, between these three disorders.

Agoraphobia

The word *agoraphobia* comes from the Greek words *agora* and *phobia*, and literally means a fear of open spaces. From an evolutionary standpoint, a fear of open spaces makes sense. Back when early humans had to regularly contend with predators, an open space was one of the most vulnerable places to be. Agoraphobia is not a specific phobia, but a complex anxiety disorder that is often accompanied by panic attacks or panic disorder.

Agoraphobia, then, is a fear of crowds and situations that are out of someone's control. The feeling of being helpless is accompanied by panic or anxiety. Ultimately, the person avoids open or public places, or other situations that cause panic. Someone with agoraphobia might be frightened of riding a bus, being in a new neighborhood, standing in line at a supermarket, or going to the movies. Most fears involve crowds and not being able to get out of a place or situation easily. This causes a person with agoraphobia extreme anxiety.

According to a National Institute of Mental Health (NIMH) survey, an estimated 2.4 percent of adolescents from thirteen to eighteen years old have agoraphobia. And the incidence among females, compared to males, is 3.4 percent higher. Most people with agoraphobia first experience panic attacks and then feel anxiety about whether the attacks will happen again. Other typical symptoms of agoraphobia include the fear of large crowded spaces, such as concerts or school hallways; closed-in spaces with many people, such as elevators and movie theaters; open spaces such as parking lots and bridges; and public transportation such as buses or trains.

All of these situations imply a lack of control in the environment. To avoid possibly having another panic attack, people with agoraphobia practice avoidance and retreat into spaces that are under their control. Panic disorder and agoraphobia often go hand-in-hand.

Social Anxiety Disorder

People with SAD experience a persistent, all-consuming fear that people are watching and judging them. A teen struggling with SAD describes her experience as if every day of school were the first day all over again. She can't find her voice, nobody picks her for group work, and she longs for someone to sit with at lunch. If a teacher calls on her, she can't bring herself to speak out. It's as if SAD is its own person, inhabiting her body. While many teens can feel these same fears, people with SAD experience the fear to an extreme degree. They can feel fear in almost any social situation and will often avoid

People with SAD are often uncomfortable in social situations. They may avoid talking to friends or meeting new people.

meeting new people or looking people in the eye. Everyday things, such as eating or going to a public restroom, become terrifying moments. Others who have SAD experience performance anxiety or stage fright.

People with SAD fear being rejected or embarrassed. They might experience physiological fear responses in social situations, such as having a tense posture. Some people might speak in a very quiet voice and be awkward and embarrassed in front of others.

Because SAD often starts in childhood with very shy children, it can go undiagnosed for years. But it's a very common anxiety disorder. According to NIMH, approximately 7 percent of Americans are affected by SAD.

Specific Phobia

Martina and Ryan aren't alone. Specific phobias are the most common type of anxiety disorder. They have an average onset age of seven years old. According to NIMH, the prevalence of specific phobias in teens is 19.3 percent, with 0.6 percent having severe impairment. Specific phobias are grouped into five different categories: animal, nature, situational, blood-injection-injury (BII), and other.

Phobias of animals are very common. In fact, 40 percent of phobic stimuli are related to bugs, spiders, mice, snakes, and bats. An animal phobia may be due to a traumatic experience as a child or young adult, but it may also not have an obvious cause. These phobias often develop in early childhood. Young children often develop phobias of natural events or environments, such as thunderstorms, heights, and open water. It is possible for these phobias to disappear with age, but according to the *DSM-5*, phobias that "persist into adulthood are unlikely to remit for the majority of individuals."[16] Some situational phobias include small spaces, the dark, and school. Claustrophobia, the fear of small spaces, is one of the most common phobias.

Many people do not like needles, blood, or medical procedures. However, upon seeing blood, or even a needle, someone with BII doesn't have the typical fear response. Instead of adrenaline, a person with BII might experience a rest and digest response. This "rest and digest" response can cause dizziness, sweatiness, tunnel vision, nausea, and fainting—similar to what we experience when we get dizzy from being hungry or standing up suddenly.

The last category of specific phobias, *other*, is less straightforward. It includes fears that cannot be grouped into the other specific phobia categories, such as a fear of swallowing or choking, or a fear of vomiting. These can be so traumatic that people with these phobias suffer from malnutrition. These fears are not to be confused with eating disorders such as anorexia or bulimia, which can manifest as an avoidance of food.

Phobias can be complex and debilitating. Consider the following experiences and feelings reported by people living with a phobia:

"I get an adrenaline rush and my heart starts pounding when I'm called on. I instantly lose my train of thought, and my words become incoherent."[17]

"Another day coming to an end and once again I feel like I've just survived. Barely breathing. Beating myself up over an illness I don't understand. . . . I would like to tell my brain to be quiet. It never listens."[18]

"I rarely leave the house, in fear I will become sick. My friendships and relationship [are] struggling because of this. . . . I'm very depressed and very alone."[19]

> "I get an adrenaline rush and my heart starts pounding when I'm called on. I instantly lose my train of thought, and my words become incoherent."[17]
>
> —*Phobia sufferer*

Understanding phobias can, perhaps, be a first positive step toward managing this disorder or being an advocate for people who live with it.

Chapter 2

DIAGNOSING PHOBIAS

Because it's such a universal experience, fear has captivated the imaginations of writers, filmmakers, and artists throughout history. Alfred Hitchcock, the director of many acclaimed thriller and horror films, made a living out of fear. In his 1955 television show, *Alfred Hitchcock Presents*, Hitchcock said, "Fear isn't so difficult to understand. . . . This fright complex is rooted in every individual."[20] Wes Craven, celebrated director of horror films such as 1984's *A Nightmare on Elm Street*, stated, "Horror films don't create fear. They release it."[21]

People who seek out fear in horror movies retain some control over their experience of fear. They can choose to turn off the movie or change the channel if the fear becomes overwhelming. But people with phobias cannot control their fear. Specific phobia, agoraphobia, and SAD are all classified as anxiety disorders in the *DSM-5*, along with other disorders such as panic disorder and generalized anxiety disorder. People who experience phobias react with significant fear when encountering their phobic stimuli, and they have significant anxiety when thinking about their phobic stimuli.

"Horror films don't create fear. They release it"[21]

—*Wes Craven, horror film director*

Everyone has felt anxious about something, probably even in the past week. Someone might have trouble sleeping the night before taking a test, playing in a big game, or appearing in a concert. She might miss her "best shot" during basketball tryouts, the ball slipping from her trembling hands. These jitters, like fear, are a normal and necessary part of life. Dr. Steimer explains that the physiological effects of anxiety help us perform better in the future. They provide coping strategies for adverse environments or situations. But people with anxiety disorders experience extreme forms of fear and anxiety, and they may avoid situations known to trigger these feelings.

For instance, it's common for people to feel uncomfortable talking in public. Before a presentation, someone might get sweaty palms and butterflies. His voice might shake while giving the presentation. But someone with a phobia of public speaking might call in sick, refuse to complete the presentation, or avoid jobs that would involve speaking in public. The first situation is healthy anxiety and fear, while the second is a crippling phobia.

How Are Phobias Diagnosed?

Some diseases have a clear pathogen. Mosquitoes carry malaria, Zika, and chikungunya. Mononucleosis is spread through contact

Many people seek out fear in horror movies. In 2017, horror movies grossed $733 million in ticket sales.

with saliva. Thanks to advances in science, some diseases can be pinpointed down to a chromosome. A mutation in the HTT gene causes Huntington's Disease. A genetic chromosome 21 disorder causes Down syndrome.

While scientists haven't discovered a "phobia gene" that causes phobias in certain people, diagnosing a specific phobia is not guesswork. It is based on clear parameters outlined in the *DSM-5*. The *DSM-5* establishes diagnostic criteria for all mental health practitioners, making both diagnosis and treatment of mental illnesses more reliable.

The *DSM* updates every few years with a new edition so diagnoses can evolve over time. For instance, in the *DSM-4* an adult had to recognize their fear or anxiety was unreasonable or excessive. In the *DSM-5* the adult doesn't need to recognize that the fear is excessive, as long as the mental health provider sees that it is. Moreover, symptoms now have to be present for six months for all ages, not just children, in order for someone to be diagnosed with a phobia.

Accurately diagnosing anxiety disorders, including phobias, is fundamental. Anxiety disorders are the "most common mental illness" in the United States, according to the ADAA.[22] NIMH reported that 19 percent of adults and nearly 32 percent of adolescents ages thirteen to eighteen experienced anxiety, and an estimated 19.3 percent of adolescents experienced specific phobia.

What Are the Diagnostic Criteria?

According to the *DSM-5*, there are seven criteria for diagnosing someone with specific phobia:

A. Marked fear or anxiety about a specific object or situation (e.g., flying, heights, animals, receiving an injection, seeing blood).

B. The phobic object or situation almost always provokes immediate fear or anxiety.

C. The phobic object or situation is actively avoided or endured with intense fear or anxiety.

D. The fear or anxiety is out of proportion to the actual danger posed by the specific object or situation and to the sociocultural context.

E. The fear, anxiety, or avoidance is persistent, typically lasting for six months or more.

F. The fear, anxiety, or avoidance causes clinically significant distress or impairment in social, occupational, or other important areas of functioning.

G. The disturbance is not better explained by the symptoms of another mental disorder.[23]

But what causes phobias? Scientists, clinicians, and researchers are exploring and better understanding the causes of phobias in order to better treat them.

There may not be a specific reason as to why a person might develop a phobia. Some people in the same family experience severe anxiety while others might not have any at all. Scientists believe phobias develop because a genetic or biological predisposition interacts with experiences that encourage the learning of fear.

Environmental Experiences

Specific phobias may link back to childhood or adolescent trauma, though they do not always have a clear cause. First, post-traumatic stress disorder (PTSD) has to be considered as a diagnosis. Once that is ruled out, a diagnosis of specific phobia is attained. Psychiatrist Dr. Michael J. Mufson says, "Growing evidence suggests highly stressful experiences, especially early in life, increase the risk for anxiety by impairing a person's ability to negotiate emotional bumps in the road later on."[24]

Part of human development includes the ability to put fears and threats in context. When a child experiences trauma, such as almost drowning or being hit by a car, this development might be skewed. Imagine two children are attacked by a vicious dog. One child develops a specific phobia of dogs and cries every time he sees a dog. But the other child does not develop the same phobia. In fact, a year later she adopts a rescue dog from a shelter. According to the Centers for Disease Control and Prevention, approximately 4.5 million Americans are bitten by dogs each year. If all victims of dog bites developed a phobia, there would be millions of Americans who have a fear of dogs. But this is not the case. So what makes one person develop a phobia and another not?

> "Growing evidence suggests highly stressful experiences, especially early in life, increase the risk for anxiety by impairing a person's ability to negotiate emotional bumps in the road later on."[24]
>
> —Dr. Michael J. Mufson, psychiatrist

It's not only the traumatic experience that can imprint the amygdala, but our social context, psychological state of mind, upbringing, genetics, environment, and other risk factors. They combine to make a person more vulnerable to developing a phobia.

Learning to Be Afraid

Aida Gómez-Robles, an anthropologist at George Washington University, explains that though brain size is inheritable in species, the organization of the cerebral cortex is much less genetically controlled. This means humans have a longer period of time than other mammals in which our brains can be shaped by the environment. This is called plasticity—the way our brains can be molded over time. Plasticity can play a significant role in the development of phobias. The brain might be molded by a traumatic event to develop a phobia of the traumatic situation or phobic stimulus.

Learning Theories and Social Acquisition of Fear

There are historically good reasons to be afraid of snakes, open spaces, and other common phobias. There are twenty-one species of venomous snakes in the United States alone. And open spaces meant vulnerability to predators for early humans. However, when these fears are taken out of context and become unreasonable, they can affect the lives of people in profound and debilitating ways—in particular, someone struggling to overcome a phobia.

Learned fear can lead to the most common specific phobias. Though scientists argue that we have an evolutionary predisposition to being afraid of creepy, crawly creatures, a Queensland University study revealed a lot of these fears have to do with association. Association means that a person holds a belief about a thing, place, or kind of person because of something she has heard, seen, or experienced. Associations can also develop through information people receive through the media, social circles, and family members. Dr. Helena Purkis says, "People tend to be exposed to a lot of negative information regarding snakes and spiders, and we argue this makes them more likely to be associated with phobia."[25] Someone who has never seen a snake in person might develop a fear of snakes from hearing other people describe snakes as evil.

The 1975 movie *Jaws* is responsible for many people's fears of sharks and shark attacks. James Hambrick, a senior clinical psychologist at the Columbia University Clinic for Anxiety and Related Disorders, works with patients with phobias. He has discussed his own fear of sharks after watching *Jaws*:

> Jaws *was a source of my own shark phobia. . . . I'm pretty sure I saw it at home on TV the first time. I remember watching most of it from behind a couch. . . . When you go out into the water, there's this idea you're incredibly vulnerable. Literally anything can kind of happen. We're built to kind of fear that, we're built to fear the unknown.*[26]

Most people never encounter a shark in real life. And sharks are not vicious, vengeful animals. The United States only averages nineteen shark attacks per year. Yet because of the popularity of *Jaws*, and more recent horror movies such as *The Shallows* and *47 Meters Down*, many people stay out of the ocean due to a phobia of shark attacks.

"*Jaws* was a source of my own shark phobia. . . . When you go out into the water, there's this idea you're incredibly vulnerable. Literally anything can kind of happen. We're built to kind of fear that, we're built to fear the unknown."[26]

—James Hambrick, senior clinical psychologist, Columbia University Clinic for Anxiety and Related Disorders

Phobias of sharks, or any other phobic stimuli, can be learned through something known as fear acquisition. There are three pathways psychiatrists and psychologists consider for learning fear acquisition: classical conditioning, operant conditioning, and vicarious conditioning.

Classical Conditioning

The idea of classical conditioning was developed by Dr. John Watson in the 1920s. He believed that all personality traits or mental disorders are a result of learning and environment. Classical conditioning is based on patterns of stimulus and response. If a child is bitten by a dog (stimulus), she might have acute fear (response). Or if a teenager has a car accident (stimulus), he might develop a fear of driving (response). Car accident statistics involving teens are alarming. In the United States, in 2015, 2,333 teens ages sixteen to nineteen were killed and 235,845 were treated in emergency rooms for injuries suffered in motor vehicle crashes. One might expect that many people develop phobias of dogs or driving; however, neither are among the most common specific phobias.

A phobia doesn't necessarily happen after one episode. If the child is exposed to the same mean dog over a period of time and feels the same fear response she did after the first attack, she might develop a phobia. Then, she would avoid dogs to avoid the fear response. For some children, it might just take one dog attack to develop a fear of dogs because of other genetic and environmental factors. The human mind is much more complex than a simple stimulus-response.

Operant Conditioning

Psychologist B.F. Skinner is regarded as the father of operant conditioning. He believed classical conditioning was too simplistic. According to operant conditioning, people repeat behaviors when the outcome is pleasurable. And people avoid repeating behaviors when the outcome is unpleasant. For example, a dog learns how to sit on command because the word *sit*, and the action of sitting down is

Specific Phobia in the Media

Hollywood has a fascination with mental illness. And specific phobias haven't escaped its lens. Examples ranging from Indiana Jones's fear of snakes to Wolverine's fear of flying have played a part in developing popular characters. A more in-depth expression of specific phobia can be seen in the character of Scottie Ferguson from Hitchcock's *Vertigo*. Ferguson has a crippling phobia of heights. He develops this phobia after watching a colleague plunge to his death. Ferguson's phobia becomes central to the plot of the story.

But sometimes Hollywood can do more harm than good when it comes to portraying mental illnesses. Ramani Durvasula, a clinical psychologist, says, "Saying a character is mentally ill . . . becomes a story device to have that person behave badly 'for a reason' and rationalizes their bad behavior . . . which further stigmatizes mental illness." Mental illnesses might even be a punch line, such as Sheldon Cooper's phobia of birds in *The Big Bang Theory*.

There is hope. Screenwriters in film and television are starting to create more nuanced, interesting characters that realistically depict what it's like to live with mental health issues. The Voice Awards program recognizes film and TV for accurately portraying mental illnesses. In 2017, winners included *Jane the Virgin* and *One Day At A Time* for portraying PTSD, addiction, and recovery storylines without stigma.

Kandra Polatis, "How TV Is Changing the Perception of Mental Disorders," *Carbondale Times*, April 15, 2014. carbondaletimes.com.

followed by praise or a treat. After a while, the dog does not need the treat to associate *sit* with a pleasurable action.

But how does operant conditioning relate to phobias? Let's say that someone crashes his car while driving. Every time he drives after the accident, he experiences a fear response, such as an increased heart rate or nausea. He begins to avoid driving to avoid the fear response that he now associates with the action. Eventually, he stops driving entirely, and relies solely on public transportation, biking, or walking to work. People with phobias often practice avoidance of their phobic stimuli to avoid the fear and anxiety that the stimuli create.

Someone with a phobia of driving may freeze every time he attempts to drive. Because of this, he may want to take public transportation instead.

Vicarious Conditioning

In the late 1970s the body of knowledge of social learning theory was expanded on by Dr. Albert Bandura and Dr. Stanley Rachman, who introduced the idea of vicarious conditioning. Vicarious conditioning helps researchers better understand and explain the development of specific phobias.

For an animal to adapt to unpredictable circumstances and environments and survive, it requires the ability to learn from personal experience as well as the experiences of others. Vicarious conditioning refers to learning as a result of consequences. Does this mean that fear is contagious?

When we think about something being "contagious," we might think about chicken pox or the flu. But fear, too, can be passed from person to person. When afraid, humans release chemical signals in our sweat. Host Anna Rothschild explains this phenomenon in an episode of *Gross Science* on PBS:

> *Humans are social beings, and we tend to mimic the feelings of those around us. This is called "emotional contagion," and it can spread either positive or negative emotions through a group. So, for instance, if you see your friend smiling, you're more likely to smile too. And vice versa. And now, thanks to the digital age, we can rapidly transmit these feelings on a global scale.*[27]

Harvard Medical School scientist Nouchine Hadjikhani and her associates study the "emotional contagion" that Rothschild describes, specifically the contagion of fear. In a 2005 poll, terrorist attacks, war, and nuclear weapons topped teens' lists of fears—though most teens had never had direct experience with any of the three. Hadjikhani's study found "humans, like other animals,

> "Humans are social beings, and we tend to mimic the feelings of those around us. This is called "emotional contagion," and it can spread either positive or negative emotions through a group. So, for instance, if you see your friend smiling, you're more likely to smile too."[27]
>
> —*Anna Rothschild, host, Gross Science*

can experience fear indirectly, the result of another's glance or muscle tensing."[28]

Further studies revealed that reinforced vicarious behavior played a significant role in fear acquisition. The results of a study conducted on forty children suggested that parents who showed fear more often had more fearful children. A parent who is afraid of flying might consciously or subconsciously teach his children to be afraid of flying. However, a parent who remains calm while flying might help a child get over his or her fear of flying before it develops into a phobia. It is possible, however, that some people will develop a phobia regardless of their social conditioning.

What Is a Genetic Predisposition to Phobia?

As far as we know, there's no such thing as a fear gene. But there have been some intriguing developments linking fear to genetics. Researchers at the Emory University School of Medicine used electric shocks on mice before allowing them to breed, while filling the air with the smell of cherry blossoms. The next generation of mice, having never been exposed to this conditioned behavior, also feared the smell of cherry blossoms, as did the following generation.

The fear became imprinted on the genome, causing structural changes in the areas that detect odor. Researchers discovered that "mice can pass on learned information about traumatic or stressful experiences—in this case a fear of the smell of cherry blossom—to subsequent generations."[29] This is an incredibly powerful study that suggests fear can physiologically change a person's genomes and structures, and then be passed on to other generations.

Genes and their different combinations and sequences are what make us unique—giving us brown hair, personality characteristics, and predispositions for certain diseases. Dr. Ian Cowell from the Institute for Cell and Molecular Biosciences at the University of Newcastle-Upon-Tyne states that "while traditional genetics describes the way the DNA sequences in our genes are passed from one generation to the next, epigenetics describes passing on the way the genes are used."[30]

Epigenes are genes that turn on or off gene segments. If genes are the script that gives our body its directions, epigenes are the directors that can call the shots. This means that even though two people share the same gene sequences, they might not be exactly the same, because their epigenes might turn certain sequences on or off.

> "[W]hile traditional genetics describes the way the DNA sequences in our genes are passed from one generation to the next, epigenetics describes passing on the way the genes are used."[30]
>
> *—Dr. Ian Cowell, Institute for Cell and Molecular Biosciences at the University of Newcastle-Upon-Tyne*

In an article published in *Pharmacology Biochemistry and Behavior*, researchers state that "[t]he human literature is in its infancy but does reveal some epigenetic associations with anxiety behaviors and disorders."[31] This body of study is still new and has a lot of detractors. Nevertheless, researcher Dr. Eric Nestler writes that "growing evidence supports a role for epigenetic regulation as a key mechanism underlying lifelong regulation of gene expression that mediates stress vulnerability."[32]

This means that scientific evidence suggests that epigenetics plays a significant role in someone's biological predisposition to develop anxiety and/or a specific phobia.

The exact size of the role that genetics plays in the development of phobias is unclear. Through new lines of study and research, like epigenetics, scientists are learning more about the intricacies of the brain and the hereditary possibilities of developing a phobia.

Scientists have also learned that once fear is implanted in the brain, it's really difficult to overcome. Stephen Johnson writes in "Fear in the Brain" that "Some scientists believe the amygdala doesn't have its own discrete storage system for emotionally charged memories but rather marks memories created by other brain systems as being somehow emotionally significant."[33] This is the way the brain becomes selective about memory—like a physiological way to highlight the significance of emotionally heavy moments. Johnson further writes, "The brain seems to be wired to prevent the deliberate overriding of fear responses."[34]

> "The brain seems to be wired to prevent the deliberate overriding of fear responses."[34]
>
> —Stephen Johnson, author of "Fear in the Brain"

When LeDoux hypothesized the two roads of fear, he realized that fear, once embedded, is incredibly difficult to eradicate. And though someone might not be conscious of why they fear something, these memories might be embedded deep in the brain. The brain's memory system is incredibly complex. There are systems dedicated to explicit memories (a memory of a childhood birthday party), procedural memories (muscle memory, such as riding a bicycle), and emotional memories.

If a person stands on a creaky bridge that feels unsafe, they may develop a fear of heights. There's an explicit memory of the event—standing on the bridge, the unsteadiness, the speed of the wind. This memory goes to the hippocampus to be put into context. But there is also an emotional memory of the event, which goes to the amygdala. The emotional memory might be the feeling of terror experienced while standing on the bridge. While thinking about heights, a person might not recall the memory of standing on the creaky bridge, but they may feel the same terror that they experienced while the event was happening. But how many of these imprints are passed on from generation to generation is unclear.

Risk Factors

By understanding the causes of anxiety disorders, it's easier to detect risk factors. Just as some people are more at risk for developing diabetes or cardiovascular problems because of genetics, environment, and lifestyle, so, too, are some people more at risk for developing phobias. Some specific risk factors include:

- Age: Specific phobias appear in early childhood, usually by age ten. Some situational phobias can develop during early adulthood.

- Gender: Women are more frequently affected by specific phobias, though according to the *DSM-5* these rates are different for all phobic stimuli. For example, animal phobias are mostly experienced by women, but BII phobia is "experienced nearly equally by both genders."[35]

- Family history: If someone in the family has a specific phobia, in particular a first-degree relative with a specific phobia, the person is more likely to develop it.

- Environment: Environmental risk factors include helicopter parents, the separation from or loss of a parent, or being physically or sexually abused as a child, all of which can lead to developing specific phobias and other anxiety disorders.

- A negative experience: A medical professional will first want to rule out PTSD in the instance of fear arising from a traumatic experience. That said, if someone has a negative experience, or has had several negative experiences, it is possible he will develop a specific phobia.

No matter how harmless the feared thing may seem to be, for someone who deals with a phobia, the fear reaction is as real as if the person were thrown into a life-or-death situation. It is threatening. It is intense. It is terrifying. And it's not always something someone expects.

Andrea shared her first experience with claustrophobia. She was happy, going on a vacation with her partner and his son to France. To pass from England to France, there's an underwater tunnel that stretches 31 miles (50 km). She'd fallen asleep before entering the tunnel. She writes:

[As] the car entered the transporter carriage, something woke me suddenly. All I could see was metal. Above us, and to both sides, walls were closing in. Stuck in a row of cars and surrounded by a safety cage, I would soon be under the sea. No way out. Completely, utterly, totally trapped.

A fireball of terror ripped upwards from my belly through my diaphragm and into my chest. Still three-quarters asleep, I screamed and fumbled frantically for the door handle as another metal grid came down around the vehicle behind us. . . . I had never experienced claustrophobia before. I collapsed in tears, my heart racing, breathing wrecked, mind cleared of everything except an appalling sense of dread.[36]

Phobias can have life-altering effects on work, school, relationships, and health. Understanding phobias and how people live with them can help someone become a better mental health advocate.

> **"Still three-quarters asleep, I screamed and fumbled frantically for the door handle as another metal grid came down around the vehicle behind us. . . . I had never experienced claustrophobia before. I collapsed in tears, my heart racing, breathing wrecked, mind cleared of everything except an appalling sense of dread."**[36]
>
> *—Andrea, a person with claustrophobia*

Chapter 3

HOW DO PHOBIAS AFFECT DAILY LIFE?

Allen Shawn, author of *Wish I Could Be There: Notes from a Phobic Life*, refers to his episodes with phobia in three stages: dread, the fear response, and a period of recovery, which can linger longer after the panic attack or moment of fear has taken place. The cycle is accompanied by feelings of great shame or embarrassment because the person experiencing the phobia is often aware it doesn't make sense. A phobia, then, can feel like it's in control of someone's life.

Karen Pickett, a psychotherapist in Los Angeles, California, shared her story about her fear of being alone with *W Magazine*. Pickett's phobia was so overwhelming that it dictated where she slept. She said: "My dad took off for a long time and my mom got involved with her new life. . . . No one was around to help me. Looking back, I see that [my phobia] was a fear of repeating what I experienced as a child."[37] Pickett initially suffered panic attacks just by thinking of going in public. Then it got worse. If Pickett didn't have anyone staying with her, she'd drive to the nearest hospital and sleep in her car. She said, "Hospitals came to represent a security that someone would help me if I felt like I was going to die."[38]

> "My dad took off for a long time and my mom got involved with her new life. . . . No one was around to help me. Looking back, I see that [my phobia] was a fear of repeating what I experienced as a child."[37]
>
> —Karen Pickett, psychotherapist

People affected by phobias can live in an exhausting state of constant alert. Nobody likes that feeling, so people affected by phobias will do almost anything to avoid it. Two of the biggest coping mechanisms of people living with phobias are avoidance coping and safety behaviors.

Avoidance

Vix [last name withheld] lives with a specific phobia. She writes, "It's almost as if someone inside takes over and I can't control myself. . . . I don't want to impose my phobia on strangers, so I control it by taking myself out of the situation."[39]

It makes sense that someone would avoid a situation that leads to a panic attack. Once the body experiences an extreme fear reaction, it attempts to avoid that reaction at all costs. But avoidance significantly alters the way people live. The *DSM-5* describes it as *active avoidance*. In active avoidance, "the individual intentionally behaves in ways that are designed to prevent or minimize contact with phobic objects or situations."[40] A person who has a phobia of heights may drive forty-five minutes out of her way to find a route to work that does not pass over a bridge. Or, she may only seek apartments on the first floor of a building, severely limiting her housing options. A person who has a phobia of blood or injections may avoid going to the doctor or seeking medical attention in an emergency.

According to the website AnxietyBC, "Avoidance is one of many survival mechanisms designed to protect us from danger."[41] But too much avoidance can be harmful. The more somebody avoids a situation or thing, the more the body registers that same situation or thing as dangerous. What was once a trace of fear in the brain worsens over time. Avoidance, though a reasonable short-term response, can unfortunately increase the severity of the phobia.

By avoiding the phobic stimulus, however, the person with a phobia is able to reduce the daily amount of fear or anxiety. Someone might be tempted to take an extreme measure, such as moving to a location with fewer snakes. Unfortunately, avoidance is not always possible, and often people have to cope using safety behaviors when faced with a phobic stimulus.

Safety Behaviors

Safety behaviors are ways a person who experiences a phobia copes with the situation. These behaviors can be anything from not leaving the house alone to always sitting in the back of a meeting.

They often help the person sidestep the phobia. Dr. Craig D. Marker, Chair of Psychology at Keiser University and founder of the Anxiety Treatment Clinic, explains, "These safety behaviors make the person feel more comfortable in the situation by providing temporary relief from anxiety. However, safety behaviors have been described as the major cause of persisting anxiety and the reason why people don't feel relief during exposures."[42] The phobia is never dealt with head on.

> "[S]afety behaviors have been described as the major cause of persisting anxiety and the reason why people don't feel relief during exposures."[42]
>
> —Dr. Craig D. Marker, Chair of Psychology, Keiser University

Exposure therapy is a common way to help people confront phobias. This type of therapy slowly introduces the person to their phobic stimuli over time, reducing the fear and anxiety associated with the phobic stimuli. But people with specific phobia often become adept at creating safety behaviors that provide momentary relief from the phobia during exposures. For example, a person with agoraphobia is supposed to attend work meetings in person as opposed to calling in or using a video chat service that she has used in the past. She attends the meeting but stands by the exit, and she does not contribute to the conversation. While she is being exposed to the phobic stimulus, the safety behavior (standing near the door) that is reducing her anxiety is not helping her overcome the phobia. These safety behaviors end up perpetuating and reinforcing the phobia, preventing the disconfirmation of fears.

Exposure therapy helps a person slowly interact with his or her phobia. For a person with a phobia of flying, one part might include standing in an airport.

Avoiding a phobia or performing safety behaviors to sidestep it can have a profound effect on the everyday lives of people who live with phobias and their families, friends, and coworkers. It can almost feel like life takes a back seat to the phobia itself, as phobias become center stage and dictate even the smallest decision.

Living with Agoraphobia

Claire Ledger, a young woman from the United Kingdom, experienced her first panic attack while shopping at a local store. Confused and afraid of the situation, Ledger began to avoid the location where she had the panic attack. But when she continued to have panic attacks in other places, she stopped traveling anywhere, even to places where she thought panic attacks *might* occur. Within five months, Ledger quit her job and was homebound. She didn't leave the house for more than two years. Ledger explained,

I got to a point where my stomach dropped as soon as I woke up. It's like a feeling of grief and despair. You're shaking, tired, and you don't really feel there. It's like you're watching yourself.

I tried to get through it, but I reached a stage when even the thought of going into my own garden made me panic. It was like coming up against an invisible wall.[43]

Eventually, Ledger began using cognitive behavioral therapy (CBT) and the help of her friends to manage her agoraphobia. Before leaving the house, she called a friend she had made in an online support group for people with agoraphobia. Ledger said, "Even though she wasn't there in person, her voice was really reassuring."[44] Thanks to coping strategies, Ledger returned to work and gained confidence about leaving the house.

But not all people with agoraphobia are housebound at some point in their lives. Composer Allen Shawn describes the limitations his agoraphobia places on his life and the elaborate mechanisms he employs to get through it. Unlike many who are affected by the disorder, Shawn manages to travel. But in order to travel, Shawn must practice his itineraries over and over again. It causes him both fear and anxiety. For example, the strain and anticipation of a four-hour car trip causes him to become "sad, jittery, and slightly irritable all day, grimly going through the motions of life. . . . It [became] difficult to focus on any but the most mundane tasks."[45]

When an orchestra in Syracuse, New York, played one of Shawn's pieces, he had to extensively prepare for the journey:

[It] required no less than six attempted trips in advance, as I repeatedly rejected routes one by one as intolerable, returning

49

to a point of reference that I came to know well. In an effort to keep myself together while on the road I develop a rather compulsive connection to such spots along the way . . . solid steel posts of reliability in a dangerous world. Along the way to Syracuse a McDonald's decorated in fifties-diner style became a secure foothold for me. . . . All of this would be funny were it not sad.[46]

Both Ledger's and Shawn's stories illustrate how agoraphobia can wrap its tendrils around someone's life, limiting it in such a way they might lose their jobs, miss opportunities, and compromise relationships.

Living with Specific Phobia

Though many people are nervous when they fly in airplanes, Eric [last name withheld] has a phobia of flying. In fact, he describes it as being "scared to death." According to AnxietyBC, Eric is "convinced that [the plane] is going to crash" any time the plane experiences turbulence.[47] He has now stopped flying completely to avoid having a panic attack on the plane. Because of this, he has missed job opportunities and promotions that would require him to travel. He has also missed out on important life moments, such as attending his sister's wedding, because it required him to travel.

John Sanford has a phobia of blood. In his book *Blood, Sweat, and Fears: A Common Phobia's Odd Pathophysiology*, he states: "[W]hat I have always found puzzling about my phobia is this: I'm not consciously afraid of blood; it just makes me feel sick."[48] Someone with a BII phobia might avoid treatment if it will require a shot or blood draw. They may even forego important medical tests. Additionally, a fear of injury might lead them to avoid all locations where they could be injured.

Michelle Clement says that just thinking about vomit can make her feel terror. She believes that her phobia of vomiting, or emetophobia, stems from a fear of losing control of her body. This phobia has caused her to avoid social situations because there's a chance that she might catch an illness from someone, which would then cause her to vomit. Clement says:

> That loss of control is not just unpleasant, it is entirely unbearable and intolerable, and the mere thought of losing control in such a manner is enough to arouse panic and hysteria. As a result, an emetophobe becomes hyperalert to internal and external cues that vomiting is about to happen. . . . As a result of this state of being hyperalert, there are undoubtedly a lot of false positives. . . . Non-pathological sensations like having gas or feeling full are misinterpreted as nausea. Nausea (real or perceived) causes anxiety, and one of the symptoms of anxiety is, yeah, more nausea. It becomes a terrible positive feedback loop that can be really hard to escape once the ball is rolling.[49]

Karen [last name withheld] was attacked by a neighbor's dog when she was a child. As a result, she developed a phobia of dogs. Not only does she avoid places

"That loss of control is not just unpleasant, it is entirely unbearable and intolerable, and the mere thought of losing control in such a manner is enough to arouse panic and hysteria."[49]

—Michelle Clement, person with emetophobia

where dogs might be, such as public parks or festivals, she also avoids photographs of dogs. Karen has had panic attacks when dogs have walked past her parked car or when a dog was sitting outside a grocery store. Her phobia has also affected her relationships with peers. Karen made her husband give away his dog before they got married. This has put a huge strain on their relationship.

Living with SAD

Any and every social situation can send someone with SAD into a cycle of dread, avoidance, fear, anxiety, and self-doubt. The show doesn't always go on.

Ricky Williams, a professional football player who played in the NFL from 1999–2011, shared his personal story and battle with SAD with the ADAA. Even though he was making millions of dollars, the pressure to perform and be in front of the cameras took a toll on his relationships with his family and the public. A simple trip to the grocery store was a struggle. He said, "I felt extremely isolated from my friends and family because I couldn't explain to them what I was feeling. I had no idea what was wrong with me."[50] His anxieties led to drug abuse and suspension from football.

In everyday life, those who live with SAD may take extreme measures to avoid things that terrify them in order to keep control of their situations. Consider these scenarios:

> "I felt extremely isolated from my friends and family because I couldn't explain to them what I was feeling. I had no idea what was wrong with me."[50]
>
> —NFL player Ricky Williams

- After drinking coffee, a teen can't bring himself to ask the waiter where the bathroom is, so he leaves the coffee shop before he planned to in order to get home and use the bathroom.

- A university student misses her first days of class because she assumes the teachers will have activities in which students will either have to introduce themselves in front of the class or mingle with other students. She would rather miss class and fall behind than have to talk to her classmates.

- After giving a presentation to the board of directors, a young woman goes home and doesn't sleep, worried that she said everything wrong and in the wrong way. She worries so much that she makes herself sick and misses two days of work. Later, she doesn't accept a promotion, as she knows she'll be expected to give even more presentations.

- A new student wants to join a club and really wants to meet people, but he's too embarrassed to ask the office about school clubs and can't bring himself to talk to any other students. He is too horrified to look people in the eye because he's sure they know that he is different.

People with SAD often express feeling isolated, strange, and disconnected, like they're not really part of this world. Because someone with SAD may feel strange and worry he might have a panic attack, he might find excuses to not go to a school dance. This can spiral into avoiding even small or low-stress social gatherings, such as a friend's house. Avoiding the situation that feels scary, in order to avoid an embarrassing panic attack, becomes more important than going to a school dance, a family reunion, or a friend's birthday party.

Share Your Story: Mental Health Awareness

Dealing with an anxiety disorder can be incredibly lonely, as there is so much misinformation about mental health. Mental health organizations like the National Alliance on Mental Illness (NAMI), Mental Health America, the ADAA and others observe Mental Health Awareness Month in May in order to better educate the public about mental health problems, provide up-to-date and accurate information about mental health, and advocate for equal care.

May was first named Mental Health Month in 1949, but misinformation is still common. One of the best ways to educate the public is by breaking the silence of mental illness. Mental Health America created the social media campaign #mentalillnessfeelslike to give voice to those who live with mental illnesses. Sharing personal stories can encourage and support other people. Some of the responses in the hashtag include:

- "Mental illness feels like trying to breathe under water. It's like you're constantly drowning and nobody can ever save you."

- "Mental illness feels like your worst enemy resides in your head, constantly telling you lies about yourself, until one day you believe them."

- "#mentalillnessfeelslike my brain has a life of its own. It twists and turns in my skull; I have no control, but I hang on to just enough of the outside world to pretend I'm OK."

Sarah Schuster, "23 Spot On Descriptions of What It's Like to Live With a Mental Illness," *The Mighty*. June 1, 2016. themighty.com

Every person's experience with phobia is unique, including how they manage it. But phobias don't exist in a bubble. Everyone who lives with anxiety and phobias can experience one or many negative social, mental, and physical health problems.

How Do Phobias Impact Relationships?

Relationships with classmates, friends, and family can suffer when someone is living with a phobia. If a friend's birthday party is at a crowded bar, a person with a phobia of enclosed spaces might skip the event. This could lead to a strained friendship or even a confrontation.

Missed school events, family reunions, or life events are almost impossible to explain. This can cause even more isolation. In Eric's story earlier, his phobia of flying caused him to miss his sister's wedding. This might cause him to become ostracized from his family or excluded from future family events.

How Do Phobias Impact School and Work?

School and work performance can suffer for someone with a phobia. In general, absenteeism is a major problem for people dealing with mental illness. A study by the World Health Organization found that mental disorders have a financial cost. "Depression and anxiety disorders cost the global economy US $1 trillion each year in lost productivity. Unemployment is a well-recognized risk factor for mental health problems."[51]

Recovering from exposure to a phobic stimulus—especially if the stimulus is present in the work or school setting—may cause people to max out their sick days or take unpaid leave. After too many absences, a person with a phobia runs the risk of failing a class or being terminated from their job. This may prevent them from graduating or finding future employment. The financial strain of missing work, as well as from medical expenses related to the phobia, can be an incredible burden. The responsibilities of supporting the person with a phobia may fall to another family member or caregiver.

People with phobias have an increased risk for developing other disorders. They may develop a substance use disorder while trying to manage their phobia.

How Do Phobias Impact Health?

Phobias are typically treated in nonmedical mental health clinics rather than medical settings, as they can have major effects on mental health. According to the *DSM-5*, "approximately 75% of people with specific phobia fear more than one situation or object" and the average person with specific phobia fears three situations or objects.[52] The more objects a person fears the harder it is to maintain a high quality of life. A person with four phobic stimuli, for example, "is likely to have more impairment in his or her occupational and social roles . . . than an individual who fears only one object or situation."[53]

Specific phobia may also increase a person's risk for other disorders, including anxiety disorders, depressive and bipolar disorders, and substance use disorders. While those with specific phobia are more likely than others to make a suicide attempt, this is most likely due to other disorders the person might have.

Phobias can also have an impact on physical health. A person with a phobia of choking or vomiting may limit the amount of foods she eats or restrict the types of foods she eats. This can lead to undernourishment. Additionally, a person with a phobia of falling or injuring himself might limit how often he walks around or gets out of bed. This can lead to muscle loss, which further restricts the person's mobility.

When the body clicks into fight-flight-freeze mode, the adrenal glands produce more cortisol. Cortisol manages the cardiovascular and circulatory system. Repeated acute stress (the fear response) or consistent chronic stress (dread or anticipatory anxiety) can cause long-term problems for the heart and blood vessels as well as the circulatory system. Phobias can also cause problems in a person's gastrointestinal (GI) tract. These might include persistent nausea, diarrhea, irritable bowels, and acid reflux.

Chapter 4

BEYOND FEAR

Phobias don't have to define a person's life. People are much more than any disorder. They are much more than a diagnosis. With the right support, access to good health care, and accurate information, phobias can be managed like any other illness.

What Are Some Techniques for Managing Phobias?

Not everyone who experiences a panic attack or has a phobia needs to see a doctor. Almost everyone will have a panic attack at some point in his or her life. In children, fear of specific objects (monsters under the bed) or situations (the dark and thunderstorms) are a universal part of growing up. There are many positive self-help techniques for coping with specific phobia and other anxiety disorders. These techniques can help result in better mental and physical health for everyone.

Information from reliable sources can be a great tool for managing phobias through education. Great resources include doctors, mental

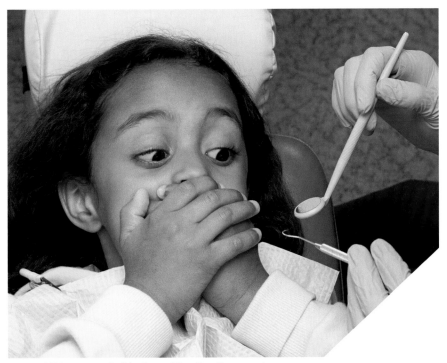

Many children are afraid of specific situations such as going to the dentist. These fears do not necessarily become phobias.

health care specialists, and counselors. NAMI, NIMH, the ADAA, and the Mayo Clinic are just a few places that provide up-to-date, accurate information about anxiety disorders and phobias.

Some lifestyle changes, such as introducing regular exercise and reducing caffeine and other stimulants, can help people manage their phobias. When adrenaline floods the body during the fight-flight-freeze response, our serotonin levels become depleted. Serotonin is a neurotransmitter that makes people feel good. Exercise and nutrition can help boost much-needed serotonin levels. Dr. Eva Selhub, a *Harvard Health* contributing editor, states that "what you eat directly effects the structure and function of your brain, and, ultimately, your mood."[54] Mary Jane Detroyer, a registered dietitian with a master's degree in Nutrition and Exercise Physiology from Columbia University, explains, "Gut health [equals] brain health because 95 [percent] of the serotonin in our bodies is produced in our guts. . . . A healthy GI tract produces more serotonin which . . . lowers anxiety and stress."[55]

Many people with anxiety disorders, including phobias, benefit from keeping journals of their fear and anxiety throughout the day. With a nutrition, exercise, or sleep diary, someone can record when her anxiety peaks and when it seems relatively low. A person can even make notes after a panic attack about what triggered the attack. This can help her productively and objectively understand the attacks.

When someone experiences anxiety or fear brought on by a phobia, he may begin to hyperventilate. This happens when the lungs take in too much oxygen, often in large, gulping breaths. The body is unable to retain the carbon dioxide it needs to properly use the oxygen. Hyperventilating can lead to symptoms like numbness, fatigue, dizziness, and shortness of breath. Learning breathing techniques, such as breathing deeply and slowly from the diaphragm, can help someone stop hyperventilating and take control of their panic. Meditation and mindfulness can also help.

Meditation is the act of sitting quietly, breathing, and focusing on the present. Techniques learned in meditation can help someone reduce daily anxiety, as well as cope with unexpected fear triggered by a phobic stimulus.

Another great strategy for people with phobias is to discuss their phobias with people who might be affected by the situation. A person who is afraid of flying or small spaces could share her fears with travel partners as well as a flight attendant before getting on the plane. Support groups are also helpful, as people with phobias can connect with others who share similar experiences. NAMI and ADAA both provide information about local groups and online forums.

If the phobia becomes unmanageable, or if someone notices that she is limiting herself based on fear, there are other alternatives. Professionals can help manage phobias and help the person find alternative solutions to dealing with her fear.

What Treatments Exist for People with Phobias?

It is important for a person with a phobia to share their experiences with a friend or trusted adult. For example, if someone has a phobia that impacts her ability to learn, she should discuss this phobia with a teacher or professor. Students, parents, and school officials can work together to create an Individualized Education Program (IEP) that provides accommodations for education. IEPs may include everything from additional test-taking time to one-on-one aides.

A general practitioner can check for any underlying medical conditions that might be causing the phobia. The doctor can also verify that what someone is feeling isn't a side effect of another medication. Once health problems are ruled out, the doctor may recommend a mental health specialist like a counselor or psychologist. A mental health provider might ask questions such as:

- Have you recently had an anxiety attack?

- How did you feel during the attack?

- What brought the attack on?

- What symptoms did you have? When did you first notice you were having these symptoms?

- When are your symptoms most likely to occur?

- What makes these symptoms better or worse?

- Have you changed your routines or habits to accommodate these symptoms? To avoid them?

- Are you taking prescription medication? Do you drink alcohol, caffeine, or take street drugs?

- Are your symptoms affecting the people in your life? Your school or work progress?

- Have you ever thought about harming yourself?

The American Psychiatric Association (APA) defines psychologists as trained professionals who "apply scientifically validated procedures to help people develop healthier, more effective habits."[56] To treat specific phobias, most psychologists use CBT. This type of therapy helps people focus on specific skills. Some CBT techniques include exposure therapy, cognitive restructuring, and mindfulness training.

Exposure therapy focuses on changing a person's response to phobic stimuli. Gradual, repeated exposure to the stimulus will help

A person with a phobia of snakes might try exposure therapy. He could look at photos of snakes before progressing to taking his own photo of a snake.

the person cope. For example, Ryan has a violent reaction to getting in an elevator. He avoids elevators whenever possible. This avoidance makes the problem worse. Exposure therapy might have him first look at pictures of an elevator. Once this trigger is mastered—once he can look at the picture of the elevator without experiencing the fear response—he will be assigned a more advanced task. This might include standing outside an elevator or even pressing the button. After he's worked up to this, the therapist might ask him to ride up one floor in an elevator with a trusted friend. Exposure therapy is like building muscles or training for a marathon. The goal of exposure therapy is not to eliminate fear, but to give someone living with a phobia the tools he needs to manage his fear.

Cognitive restructuring is the act of rewiring flawed thought processes. Many people who have specific phobia have irrational, catastrophic thoughts. Consider Karen, the woman with a phobia of dogs. She was attacked by a dog as a child and only relates them to death and terror. During cognitive restructuring, psychotherapists work with patients to recognize counterproductive thought patterns. According to Cognitive Behavioral Therapy Los Angeles, the thoughts are then replaced with "more realistic thoughts" which result in "decreased anxiety and avoidance."[57] What a therapist is doing is trying to replace automatic, flawed thought processes through a series of systematic steps.

First, the patient has to calm down. Once the fear response subsides, the therapist will ask the patient to identify the stressor. For instance, Martina will write about flying. Ryan will write about being stuck in an elevator. Once the stressor is identified, a patient should write down how the stressor makes her feel. Feelings, generally, are quite negative. They might include phrases like *scared*, *out of control*, *trapped*, *sad*, and *insecure*.

The third step is writing down the thought processes and rating how much the patient believes the automatic thought. This is that automatic running commentary that goes through our brains when we're confronted with the stimulus, such as: *I'm going to die if I go on an airplane* or *the elevator might break, and I won't be able to get out.* Then the patient will look at the list of thoughts and analyze them and how much they believe them.

Finally, the patient is asked to replace the negative thought with a more realistic thought. This might be, "I believe I'm going to die if I go on an airplane, but statistics show that air travel is one of the safest kinds of travel." Or, "I feel like I'm going to run out of air on the elevator, but I know that's impossible, because elevators aren't airtight."

The final restructuring of negative thoughts takes time. And initially, a patient might not believe the counter-thought. That said, over time, like doing exercise to develop upper body strength, the patient is working to restructure those automatic thought processes.

Mindfulness-based cognitive therapy (MBCT) is practiced by an MBCT therapist—a mental health professional who has had additional training in mindfulness practices. MBCT and CBT have some overlap, but there are very clear differences. CBT focuses on controlling negative thought processes, whereas MBCT is a much more present-based practice that focuses on acceptance of one's thoughts and feelings. The MBCT therapist's goal, then, is to help a patient change their relationship with negative feelings by practicing meditation and mindfulness.

Steps in mindfulness training include mindful breathing, simply focusing on in-breath and out-breath. The second step is concentration, following the route of the in-breath and out-breath. The third step is being aware of the body. The fourth is releasing tension in the body. And the final step is mindful walking, being aware of every step and the joy each step brings. This concentration on the basics can bring people with phobias out of the fear response state and back to the present. Dr. Elizabeth Hoge, psychiatrist and Harvard University assistant professor, explains, "People with anxiety have a problem dealing with distracting thoughts that have too much power."[58] Through breathing and meditation, mindfulness training

> **"People with anxiety have a problem dealing with distracting thoughts that have too much power."[58]**
>
> —Dr. Elizabeth Hoge, psychiatrist

One Breath at a Time

In the 1970s, Harvard Medical School cardiologist Dr. Herbert Benson developed a "relaxation response" to help manage stress cycles. Though studies have shown that relaxation techniques on their own aren't very helpful, if used in conjunction with other therapies, relaxation techniques can be helpful. The relaxation response can be achieved in a few steps:

1. Sit quietly in a comfortable position.

2. Close your eyes.

3. Starting at the feet, relax all muscles one by one.

4. Pick a short, soothing word to repeat while you breathe, such as *one* or *blue*. It should not have any negative associations. Say the word as you breathe out through your nose.

5. Continue for ten minutes. Once you are finished, remain seated with your eyes closed. Do not stand up for a few minutes, even after you open your eyes.

helps a person to reduce the noise of the fear response and tap into what's really going on.

It's important to note a particular kind of therapy and a specific therapist won't be a perfect fit for everyone. Just like people should search for the right primary care doctor to treat physical illness, people may need to try different therapists and styles of therapy until they find the right fit for them. The effectiveness of a treatment depends on a patient sticking to the treatment plan prescribed. He should practice recommended strategies to reduce anxiety, be consistent, and remember that nothing happens overnight. The more someone works with the tools a therapist or medical practitioner gives, the more likely a person will be able to make significant changes in his life.

Medication

As successful as therapy is in treating phobias, sometimes clinicians might prescribe medication to help with anxiety, panic symptoms, depression, and other possible co-occurring problems. A doctor might also prescribe a medication for very specific, short-term situations.

Before she gets on an airplane, Martina has started to take a benzodiazepine—a kind of sedative—to help her get through the trip without feeling such extreme terror. If someone suffers from claustrophobia, like Ryan, his doctor might prescribe a sedative if he needs to have tests done in a small room or machine. Medication for specific moments like this, in conjunction with therapy, can be effective. There are several different types of medications that are used to treat phobias and other anxiety disorders.

Selective serotonin reuptake inhibitors (SSRIs), such as Zoloft and Lexapro, work in the body to block the reabsorption of serotonin by the brain, making more serotonin available. Selective serotonin-norepinephrine reuptake inhibitors (SNRIs), such as Cymbalta and Effexor, are similar to SSRIs, but block the reabsorption of both serotonin and norepinephrine in the brain. Both SSRIs and SNRIs are considered a first-line treatment, as they have been proven effective in treating anxiety disorders.

Benzodiazepines, such as Xanax and Valium, are effective for short-term problems. For example, someone with a fear of flying might take a benzodiazepine before a flight. Because the body can develop a tolerance for benzodiazepines, the dose might have to

People with phobias appreciate the support of their friends and family. This might involve going with them to a crowded place or helping them start to drive again.

be increased. Over a period of a long time, this might cause addiction and more anxiety.

The Reality of Phobias

Phobias can take a toll on all relationships. They can be overwhelming. Mental health professionals are encouraging family-based treatments, so everyone is informed and can support one another. Through education, everyone can be a person of support to someone struggling with a phobia. Getting informed and becoming an advocate for mental health awareness, such as through joining NAMI or the

ADAA, could be the best way to support a loved one who is struggling with a phobia. Not judging someone when she talks about her phobia is another way to offer support. Effective listening skills include facing the speaker, being mindful of what she's saying and keeping an open mind, not interrupting or imposing solutions, and asking clarifying questions.

The responsibility to get well and heal is in the hands of the patient. But by being an advocate for mental health, listening, and setting boundaries in order to not get consumed by another person's phobia, a person can be an indispensable part of a necessary support network for someone getting treated for specific phobias and other anxiety disorders. Sometimes a person experiencing an episode with a phobia just needs to know she's not alone.

Phobias are often misunderstood, even laughed at, whether being the butt of a joke in a TV show or with a group of friends. Misconceptions are perpetuated, so the best defense is education. Phobias are real, powerful, and can affect a person's school, family, and work life, as well as their physical health. By understanding phobias, teens can practice techniques to reduce anxiety and better manage their phobias, as well as become mental health advocates for others that are struggling with a phobia.

INTRODUCTION: RYAN AND MARTINA

1. American Psychiatric Association, *Diagnostic and Statistical Manual of Mental Disorders*. Arlington, VA: American Psychiatric Publishing, 2013, p. 189.

2. Thierry Steimer, "The Biology of Fear- and Anxiety-Related Behaviors." *Dialogues in Clinical Neuroscience* 4.3 (2002): pp. 231–249.

3. "Should I Be Upfront About My Fear of Flying?" *The Guardian*, April 27, 2015. www.theguardian.com.

4. "About ADAA Facts and Statistics," *Anxiety and Depression Association of America*. n.d. www.adaa.org.

5. "About ADAA Facts and Statistics," *Anxiety and Depression Association of America*.

CHAPTER 1: WHAT ARE PHOBIAS?

6. Carlos Coelho and Helena Purkis, "The Origins of Specific Phobias: Influential Theories and Current Perspectives," Review of General Psychology 13 (2009). p. 13.

7. Shawn Allen, *Wish I Could Be There: Notes from a Phobic Life*. New York, NY: Penguin Random House, 2007.

8. Arash Javanbakht and Linda Saab, "What Happens in the Brain When We Feel Fear," *Smithsonian.com*, October 27, 2017. www.smithsonianmag.com.

9. "Understanding the Stress Response," *Harvard Health Publishing*, May 1, 2018. www.health.harvard.edu.

10. "How Your Brain Works," *Mayo Clinic*, April 20, 2016. www.mayoclinic.org.

11. Stephen Johnson, "Fear in the Brain," *Discover*, March 1, 2003. discovermagazine.com.

12. John Hawks, "How Has the Human Brain Evolved?" *Scientific American*. n.d. www.scientificamerican.com.

13. Hawks, "How Has the Human Brain Evolved?"

14. Johnson, "Fear in the Brain."

15. Johnson, "Fear in the Brain."

16. American Psychiatric Association, *Diagnostic and Statistical Manual of Mental Disorders*. Arlington, VA: American Psychiatric Publishing, 2013, p. 200.

17. "Being the Weird Kid," *Social Anxiety Support*, December 5, 2017. www.socialanxietysupport.com.

18. "This Is the Time of Day," *Phobia Support Forum*, Spetember 8, 2016. www.phobiasupport.com.

19. "Emetephobia," *Phobia Support Forum*, March 15, 2016. www.phobiasupport.com.

CHAPTER 2: DIAGNOSING PHOBIAS

20. Jeryl Brunner, "12 Quotes to Honor Alfred Hitchcock's Birthday," *Parade*, August 13, 2015. www.parade.com.

21. Sherry Phillips, "Remembering Wes Craven: The Guru of Gore's 10 Best Quotes on Filmmaking and Fear," *Parade*, August 31, 2015. www.parade.com.

22. "About ADAA Facts and Statistics," *Anxiety and Depression Association of America*.

23. American Psychiatric Association, *Diagnostic and Statistical Manual of Mental Disorders*. Arlington, VA: American Psychiatric Publishing, 2013, p. 197.

24. Michael J. Mufson, "Can a Traumatic Event Cause Anxiety Disorders?" *ShareCare*, n.d. www.sharecare.com.

25. University of Queensland, "Unlocking the Psychology of Snake and Spider Phobias," *ScienceDaily*, March 24, 2008. www.sciencedaily.com.

26. Tim Donnelly, "Why 'Jaws' Terrifies Even Phobia Experts," *New York Post*, June 18, 2015. nypost.com.

27. Anna Rothschild, *Is Fear Contagious?*, PBS, February 16, 2017. www.pbs.org.

28. Ann Marie Menting, "The Chill of Fear," *Harvard Medicine*, 2011. www.hms.harvard.edu.

29. Richard Gray, "Phobias May Be Memories Passed Down in Genes from Ancestors," *The Telegraph*, December 1, 2013. www.telegraph.co.uk.

30. Ian Cowell, "Epigenetics—It's Not Just Genes That Make Us," *British Society for Cell Biology*, n.d. www.bscb.org.

31. Steven J. Nieto et al., "Don't Worry; Be Informed About the Epigenetics of Anxiety," *Pharmacology Biochemistry and Behavior* (146–147), 2016.

32. Eric J. Nestler, "Transgenerational Epigenetic Contributions to Stress Responses: Fact or Fiction?" *PLOS Biology* 14.6 (2016): e1002486.

33. Johnson, "Fear in the Brain."

34. Johnson, "Fear in the Brain."

35. American Psychiatric Association, *Diagnostic and Statistical Manual of Mental Disorders*. Arlington, VA: American Psychiatric Publishing, 2013, p. 199.

36. Andrea Perry, "Trapped . . . Then I Discovered That I Was Claustrophobic," *The Telegraph*, March 3, 2008. www.telegraph.co.uk.

CHAPTER 3: HOW DO PHOBIAS AFFECT DAILY LIFE?

37. Emily Holt, "Me, Myself and I," *W Magazine*, December 1, 2007. www.wmagazine.com.

38. Holt, "Me, Myself and I."

39. Vix, "Living with My Phobia of Bananas," *Mind*, August 3, 2017. www.mind.org.uk.

40. American Psychiatric Association, *Diagnostic and Statistical Manual of Mental Disorders*. Arlington, VA: American Psychiatric Publishing, 2013, p. 198.

41. "Avoidance," *AnxietyBC*. n.d. www.anxietybc.com.

42. Craig D. Marker, "Safety Behaviors in Social Anxiety," *Psychology Today*, March 3, 2013. www.psychologytoday.com.

43. "Claire's Story," *NHS Choices*, February 20, 2016. www.nhs.uk.

44. "Claire's Story," *NHS Choices*.

45. Allen, *Wish I Could Be There: Notes from a Phobic Life*.

46. Allen, *Wish I Could Be There: Notes from a Phobic Life*.

47. "Specific Phobia," *AnxietyBC*. n.d. www.anxietybc.com.

48. John Sanford, "Blood, Sweat, and Fears," *Stanford Medicine*, 2013. http://sm.stanford.edu/archive/stanmed.

49. Michelle Clement, "My Experience with Emetophobia, and Some Questions for the Blogosphere," *Scientific American*, September 26, 2011. blogs.scientificamerican.com.

50. Leslie Anderson, "Ricky Williams: A Story of Social Anxiety Disorder," *Anxiety and Depression Association of America*, n.d. adaa.org.

51. "Mental Health in the Workplace," *World Health Organization*, September 2017. www.who.int.

52. American Psychiatric Association, *Diagnostic and Statistical Manual of Mental Disorders*. Arlington, VA: American Psychiatric Publishing, 2013, p. 198.

53. American Psychiatric Association, *Diagnostic and Statistical Manual of Mental Disorders*. Arlington, VA: American Psychiatric Publishing, 2013, p. 201.

CHAPTER 4: BEYOND FEAR

54. Eva Selhub, "Nutritional Psychiatry: Your Brain on Food," *Harvard Health*, November 16, 2015. www.health.harvard.edu.

55. Mary Jane Detroyer, "Observe World Mental Health Day," *Nutrition and Exercise Tips to Improve Mental Health from NYC Registered Dietitian and Personal Trainer*," October 11, 2017. www.maryjanedetroyer.com.

56. "Understanding Psychotherapy and How It Works," *American Psychological Association*, n.d. www.apa.org.

57. Cognitive Behavioral Therapy Los Angeles, "Phobia Treatment: Cognitive Behavioral Therapy," n.d. cogbtherapy.com.

58. June Corliess, "Mindfulness Meditation May Ease Anxiety, Mental Stress," *Havard Health*, January 8, 2014. www.health.harvard.edu.

BOOKS

Edmund J. Bourne, *The Anxiety and Phobia Workbook*. Oakland, CA:
New Harbinger Publications, 2015.

Elaine Chong and Erin Hovanec, *Phobias*. New York, NY:
Rosen, 2014.

Carol Hand, *Living with Anxiety Disorders*. Minneapolis, MN:
Abdo, 2017.

Bitsy Kemper, *Teens and Phobias*. San Diego, CA:
ReferencePoint Press, 2017.

Peggy J. Parks, *Anxiety Disorders*. San Diego, CA:
ReferencePoint Press, 2011.

Polly Wells, ed., *Freaking Out: Real-Life Stories About Anxiety.* Toronto, ON:
Annick Press, 2013.

INTERNET SOURCES

Tim Donnelly, "Why 'Jaws' Terrifies Even Phobia Experts," *New York Post*,
June 18, 2015. nypost.com.

Arash Javanbakht and Linda Saab, "What Happens in the Brain When We
Feel Fear," *Smithsonian.com*, October 27, 2017. smithsonian.com.

Diana Kwon, "What Makes Our Brains Special?" *Scientific American*,
November 24, 2015. scientificamerican.com.

Anna Rothschild, "Is Fear Contagious?" *NOVA*, February 16, 2017. npr.org.

WEBSITES

Anxiety.org: Phobias

www.anxiety.org/phobias

This website offers expert information about the symptoms of phobias, causes, and treatments, as well as information about other anxiety disorders.

Anxiety and Depression Association of America

adaa.org

The Anxiety and Depression Association of America helps people identify, prevent, and manage anxiety disorders such as phobias. The website offers tips for managing phobias, describes different types of phobias, and helps people find mental health and other treatment options.

The National Alliance on Mental Illness

nami.org

The National Alliance on Mental Illness is the nation's largest grassroots mental health organization. Its mission is to better the lives of millions of Americans living with mental health issues by offering accurate, up-to-date information, advocating for mental health coverage, listening to those who need to share their stories, whether online or by phone, and leading mental health initiatives.

The National Institute of Mental Health

nimh.nih.gov

The National Institute of Mental Health is the official US government site on mental health. The institute's goal is to "transform the understanding and treatment of mental illness."

INDEX

adrenal glands, 15, 16, 57

adrenaline, 15, 24, 25, 59

agoraphobia, 21–22, 26, 47, 48–50

American Psychiatric Association (APA), 62

amygdala, 13, 15, 16, 19, 20–21, 31, 40, 41

anxiety, 9, 10, 12, 13, 21, 22, 23–24, 27, 28, 29, 30, 32, 35, 39, 40, 46, 47, 49, 51, 52, 54, 57, 60–61, 64, 65, 66, 67, 68, 69

Anxiety and Depression Association of America (ADAA), 7, 8–9, 29, 52, 54, 59, 61, 69

anxiety disorders, 10, 21, 22, 24, 26–27, 29, 41, 42, 54, 55, 57, 58, 59, 60, 67, 69

AnxietyBC, 46, 50

association, 32, 39, 66

avoidance, 7, 22, 25, 30, 35, 45–46, 52, 63, 64

Bandura, Albert, Dr., 36

benzodiazepine, 67, 68

brain, 12, 13, 15, 16–21, 25, 31–32, 40, 46, 54, 59, 60, 64, 67

Centers for Disease Control and Prevention, 31

cerebellum, 19

circulatory system, 57

classical conditioning, 33–34

claustrophobia, 7–8, 24, 42–43, 67

Clement, Michelle, 51

cognitive behavioral therapy (CBT), 49, 62, 65

Cognitive Behavioral Therapy Los Angeles, 64

cognitive restructuring, 62, 63–64

coping mechanism, 27, 45, 49, 58

cortex, 19, 31

cortisol, 16, 57

Cowell, Ian, Dr., 39

Craven, Wes, 26

depression, 25, 55, 57, 67

Detroyer, Mary Jane, 59–60

Diagnostic and Statistical Manual of Mental Disorders Fifth Edition (DSM-5), 6, 24, 26, 28–29, 41, 46, 56

drug abuse, 52

emetophobia, 51

Emory University School of Medicine, 38

epigenes, 39–40

epinephrine, 15–16

exposure therapy, 47, 62–63

fear response, 8–9, 10–11, 12, 13, 15–16, 20–21, 23, 24, 34, 35, 40, 44, 57, 63, 64–66

fight-flight-freeze response, 11, 15, 19, 57, 59

flying, fear of, 6, 7, 8, 29, 35, 38, 50, 55, 61, 64, 67

gastrointestinal (GI) tract, 57
genes, 28, 30–31, 34, 38–41
genome, 38
Gómez-Robles, Aida, 31
Gross Science, 37
Guardian, the, 8

Hadjikhani, Nouchine, 37–38
Hambrick, James, 32–33
Harvard Health, 15, 59
Harvard University, 65
Hawks, John, 18–19
hippocampus, 16, 19, 41
Hitchcock, Alfred, 26
Hoge, Elizabeth, Dr., 65
hyperventilation, 60
hypothalamus, 15, 16, 19

impact on
    health, 43, 54, 54, 56–57, 58–59,
        60, 62, 69
    relationships, 25, 43, 50, 52, 55,
        65, 68
    school and work, 22, 43, 48,
        53–54, 55–56, 62, 69
imprinting, 20, 31, 38, 41
Individualization Education Program
    (IEP), 61

Jaws, 32–33
Johnson, Stephen, 17–18, 20, 40

Ledger, Claire, 48–49, 50
LeDoux, Joseph, 19–20, 40
limbic system, 15

MacLean, Paul D., Dr., 18
Marker, Craig D., Dr., 47
Mayo Clinic, 16, 59
memory, 17, 40–41
Mental Health America, 54
Mindfulness-based cognitive therapy
    (MBCT), 65
Mufson, Michael J., Dr., 30

National Institute of Mental Health
    (NIMH), 22, 24, 29, 59
National Alliance on Mental Illness
    (NAMI), 54, 59, 61, 69
nausea, 24–25, 35, 51, 57
neocortex, 19
nutrition, 25, 59–60

operant conditioning, 33, 34–35

panic attack, 21, 22, 44–45, 48, 50,
    52, 53–54, 58, 60
PBS, 37
*Pharmacology Biochemistry and
    Behavior*, 39
phobic stimulus, 7, 8, 9, 15, 24,
    32, 33, 34, 41, 46, 47, 55, 57, 61,
    62, 64
Pickett, Karen, 44–45
post-traumatic stress disorder
    (PTSD), 30, 35, 42

Rachman, Stanley, Dr., 36
risk factors, 31, 41–42, 55
Rothschild, Anna, 37

safety behaviors, 45, 46–48

Sanford, John, 50

selective serotonin reuptake inhibitor (SSRI), 67

selective serotonin-norepinephrine reuptake inhibitors (SNRI), 67

Selhub, Eva, Dr., 59–60

serotonin, 59–60, 67

Shawn, Allen, 11–12, 44, 49–50

Skinner, B.F., 34

snakes, fear of, 7, 20, 24, 32, 35, 46

social anxiety disorder (SAD), 21, 22–24, 26, 52–53

specific phobia, 7, 8, 10, 21, 24–25, 26, 28–29, 30–31, 32, 34, 35, 36, 40, 41, 42, 45, 47, 50–52, 56–57, 58, 62, 63, 69

specific phobia types
  animal, 24, 29, 33, 41
  blood-injection-injury (BII), 24, 29, 46, 50
  nature, 10, 20, 24, 29, 35, 41, 46
  other, 24, 25, 51, 57
  situational, 8, 10, 11, 21–22, 23, 24, 27, 29, 32, 41, 42, 45, 46, 52–53, 56–57, 58, 61, 67

Steimer, Thierry, Dr., 6–7, 27

stress, 11, 30, 38, 53, 57, 60, 64, 66

thalamus, 15

trauma, 17, 24, 25, 30, 31, 32, 38, 42

treatment, 9, 28, 50, 66, 67, 68

triune brain theory, 18–19

University of Queensland, 11

vicarious conditioning, 33, 36–38

Voice Awards, 35

Watson, John, Dr., 34

Wayne State University, 15

Williams, Ricky, 52

World Health Organization, 55

IMAGE CREDITS

Cover: © ArtOfPhotos/Shutterstock Images

5: © PR Image Factory/Shutterstock Images

9: © monkeybusinessimages/iStockphoto

12: © Val Thoermer/Shutterstock Images

14: © logika600/Shutterstock Images

17: © Monkey Business Images/Shutterstock Images

23: © Daisy-Daisy/iStockphoto

28: © SrdjanPav/iStockphoto

36: © anyaberkut/iStockphoto

48: © pikcha/Shutterstock Images

56: © Fred Sweet/Shutterstock Images

59: © XiXinXing/iStockphoto

63: © Ramukanji/Shutterstock Images

68: © Rawpixel/iStockphoto

ABOUT THE AUTHOR

Heidi Ayarbe is an author, storyteller, and translator. Born in Nevada, she now lives with her family in Colombia, South America, where she drinks too much coffee and misses Cheerios.